A Minimalis Frugal Living Saving Money and Enjoying Life

Copyright © 2023 by Hazel Nightingale.

All rights reserved.

No part of this book may be reproduced or transmitted in any form or by any means, electronic or mechanical, including photocopying, recording, or by any information storage and retrieval system, without permission in writing from the author.

This book was created with the assistance of an artificial intelligence program, and the author acknowledges the contributions of the program in the creation of this work.

This book is for entertainment purposes only. The information and advice contained within should not be used as a substitute for professional advice or guidance. The author and publisher are not responsible for any actions taken by the reader as a result of the information provided in this book. It is always recommended to consult with a professional in the field before making any significant changes in your life.

The Unexpected Discovery 6

Learning the Basics of Frugalism 8

The Joy of Living with Less 10

The Power of Budgeting 12

Finding the Right Mindset 14

The Secret to Frugal Grocery Shopping 16

Meal Planning on a Tight Budget 18

Reducing Waste and Saving Money 20

Simple DIY Hacks to Save Money 23

The Beauty of Thrift Store Finds 25

Prioritizing Experiences over Things 27

How to Travel on a Shoestring Budget 29

Staying Fashionable on a Frugal Budget 31

The Importance of Saving for a Rainy Day 33

Frugal Ways to Celebrate Special Occasions 35

Tips for Hosting a Frugal Party 37

Understanding Your Spending Triggers 39

Dealing with Social Pressure to Spend 41

Setting Realistic Financial Goals 43

The Benefits of a Frugal Mindset 46

Frugal Habits for a Sustainable Future 48

Overcoming the Fear of Missing Out 51

Navigating the Pitfalls of Credit Cards 53

Finding Support in Your Frugal Journey 55

Maintaining a Positive Outlook on Frugal Living 57

The Power of Gratitude in a Frugal Lifestyle 59

Coping with Setbacks and Financial Emergencies 61

Celebrating the Benefits of Frugalism 64

Conclusion 66

The Unexpected Discovery

For as long as I could remember, I had been chasing the next big purchase. It started with toys as a child, and then evolved to more expensive items as I got older. I was always on the lookout for the latest gadget, the newest fashion trend, the flashiest car. It wasn't until my mid-twenties that I stumbled upon an unexpected discovery that changed my life forever.

It happened on a day much like any other. I was browsing through my social media feed, scrolling through pictures of my friends' latest purchases, when I came across a post that caught my eye. It was a picture of a woman sitting in a minimalist living room, surrounded by only a few carefully curated items. The caption read, "Living a frugal life has brought me more joy than any material possession ever could."

I was intrigued. Up until that point, I had never considered the possibility that living a frugal lifestyle could bring happiness. I clicked on the woman's profile and began to read her story. She had once been a big spender, just like me. But she had found that constantly chasing after material possessions had left her feeling empty and unfulfilled.

As I continued to read, I started to realize that many of the things that had brought me temporary pleasure in the past had ultimately left me feeling the same way. I remembered the excitement I felt when I bought a new phone, only to feel bored with it a few weeks later. I thought about the times I had gone on extravagant vacations, only to come back feeling more stressed than ever.

I was suddenly overcome with a desire to learn more about this frugal lifestyle. I started doing research, reading blogs and watching videos about how to live a simpler, more intentional life. I learned about budgeting and meal planning, and I started to see how small changes could add up to big savings. At first, the idea of cutting back on my spending made me feel anxious. I was afraid that I wouldn't be able to maintain my lifestyle, that I would have to give up the things that I loved. But as I began to implement some of the tips I had learned, I started to feel a sense of freedom that I had never experienced before.

I started to find joy in the simple things, like cooking a meal from scratch or going for a walk in the park. I began to appreciate the items I already owned, rather than constantly feeling the need to buy more. I even started to enjoy the process of saving money, watching my bank account grow with each passing month.

Now, years later, I look back on that unexpected discovery as the turning point in my life. It was the moment that I realized that true happiness isn't found in material possessions, but in the relationships we cultivate and the experiences we have. I still have moments when I slip back into old habits, but I always come back to the lessons I learned during that transformative time.

The frugal lifestyle isn't for everyone, but for me, it has been a source of immense joy and fulfillment. I am grateful for that unexpected discovery, and for the opportunity to live a simpler, more intentional life.

Learning the Basics of Frugalism

As I delved deeper into the world of frugalism, I quickly realized that there was a lot to learn. I had always thought of myself as a relatively thrifty person, but I had never truly understood the power of frugal living until I began to explore it in earnest.

The first thing I learned was that budgeting is the cornerstone of a frugal lifestyle. I had always had a general idea of how much I spent each month, but I had never created a detailed budget that accounted for all of my expenses. When I sat down to do this for the first time, I was shocked to see how much I was spending on things like eating out and shopping.

Creating a budget forced me to confront some uncomfortable truths about my spending habits. I realized that I was using my credit card more than I should, and that I was often making impulse purchases without thinking through the consequences. But at the same time, I felt empowered by the knowledge that I now had the tools to take control of my finances.

The next thing I learned was the importance of meal planning. Before I started living a frugal lifestyle, I would often go to the grocery store without a plan and end up buying more than I needed. I would then let food go to waste because I didn't have a plan for how to use it.

Now, I create a weekly meal plan and shopping list before I go to the store. This not only helps me save money by buying only what I need, but it also helps me avoid the temptation to eat out because I have a plan for what I will eat at home.

Another important aspect of frugal living is finding ways to reduce waste. This can mean anything from composting food scraps to using reusable shopping bags. One of my personal examples of this was when I started using a reusable water bottle instead of buying disposable plastic bottles. This not only saved me money, but it also helped reduce my impact on the environment.

Frugalism also taught me the value of taking care of what I already owned. Instead of constantly buying new clothes, I started mending and repurposing the ones I already had. I also started taking better care of my possessions, whether it was by regularly cleaning my car or getting my shoes resoled instead of buying new ones.

All of these small changes added up to big savings over time. But more importantly, they helped me live a more intentional and fulfilling life. I no longer felt like I was constantly chasing after the next big purchase, but instead was content with what I had.

Learning the basics of frugalism was not always easy. It required me to confront some uncomfortable truths about my spending habits and make some significant changes in my life. But the benefits have been more than worth it. I now feel more in control of my finances, and I have a deeper appreciation for the things that truly matter in life.

The Joy of Living with Less

As I continued to embrace frugalism, I discovered something unexpected: the joy of living with less. In a society that often equates material possessions with success and happiness, it can be difficult to imagine that having less could actually lead to a more fulfilling life. But that is exactly what I found to be true.

One of the first things I did when I started living more frugally was to declutter my home. I had always been a bit of a packrat, holding onto things I didn't really need "just in case." But as I went through my possessions and got rid of the things that were no longer useful or meaningful to me, I felt a weight lifting off my shoulders.

I no longer felt weighed down by my possessions, but instead felt liberated by the space and simplicity that came with having less. I began to appreciate the things that truly mattered to me, like spending time with loved ones, pursuing my passions, and experiencing the beauty of nature.

Living with less also meant that I had more time and energy to focus on the things that really mattered. I no longer spent my weekends wandering through malls or scrolling through online shopping sites. Instead, I found joy in simple pleasures like taking a walk in the park or cooking a meal with fresh, local ingredients.

One personal example of this was when I decided to sell my car and start biking to work. I was nervous at first, worried about how I would manage in bad weather or if I had to carry something heavy. But as I got used to the routine, I found that biking to work not only saved me money on gas and parking, but it also gave me a sense of freedom and independence that I had never experienced before.

Living with less also meant that I had more financial freedom. By saving money on unnecessary purchases and focusing on the things that truly mattered, I was able to save up for things that I really wanted, like travel or investing in my education. And because I was no longer beholden to my possessions, I felt more confident in my ability to handle whatever life threw my way.

The joy of living with less is not something that can be easily quantified or measured. It is a feeling that comes from a sense of purpose and contentment that goes beyond material possessions. It is a way of living that values experiences over things, and that recognizes the beauty and simplicity that can be found in the everyday.

As I continue on my journey of frugalism, I am constantly reminded of the joy that comes from living with less. It is a lesson that I will carry with me for the rest of my life.

The Power of Budgeting

When I first began my frugal journey, I had a vague idea that I needed to save money and cut back on my spending. However, it wasn't until I discovered the power of budgeting that I truly began to make progress.

A budget is a powerful tool that can help you take control of your finances, rather than feeling like your finances are controlling you. It involves tracking your income and expenses, and creating a plan for how you will allocate your money each month.

One of the biggest benefits of budgeting is that it helps you to identify areas where you can cut back on your spending. By tracking your expenses, you can see exactly where your money is going and identify any areas of overspending. This can help you make more conscious decisions about how you spend your money, and ensure that you are prioritizing your needs and values.

For example, when I started tracking my expenses, I realized that I was spending a lot of money on dining out and takeout food. While I enjoyed the convenience and variety of restaurant meals, I realized that I was overspending on something that I could easily do myself. So I started cooking more at home, which not only saved me money but also allowed me to experiment with new recipes and flavors.

Another benefit of budgeting is that it can help you plan for the future. By allocating money towards savings or paying down debt, you can create a solid foundation for your financial future. For example, when I created my first budget, I made sure to include a line item for emerger savings. While I didn't know exactly what I would need the money for, I knew that having a cushion would give me peace of mind and protect me in case of unexpected expenses.

Finally, budgeting can be empowering. When you have a plan for your money, you feel more in control of your finances and can make intentional choices about how you want to live your life. You can save for things that are important to you, like a vacation or a new car, and feel confident that you are making progress towards your goals.

One personal example of this was when I decided to go back to school to pursue a new career. While the idea of taking on more debt was daunting, I knew that by creating a budget and making intentional choices about my spending, I could make it work. By cutting back on unnecessary expenses and allocating money towards tuition payments, I was able to achieve my goal of earning a degree without sacrificing my financial stability.

In conclusion, the power of budgeting cannot be overstated. It is a simple but effective tool that can help you take control of your finances, plan for the future, and make intentional choices about how you want to live your life. By creating a budget and sticking to it, you can achieve financial stability and freedom, and create a solid foundation for your future.

Finding the Right Mindset

When it comes to frugalism, finding the right mindset is key. It's not just about cutting back on your spending, but it's about developing a different way of thinking about money and resources.

For me, finding the right mindset meant shifting my focus from what I didn't have to what I did have. Instead of feeling deprived because I couldn't afford the latest gadgets or trendy clothes, I began to appreciate the things that I did have and find joy in the simple pleasures of life.

One way I did this was by practicing gratitude. I started a gratitude journal where I would write down three things I was thankful for each day, no matter how small they may seem. This helped me to shift my focus away from what I lacked and towards the abundance in my life, whether it was a warm cup of tea or a kind word from a friend.

Another important mindset shift for me was realizing that being frugal doesn't mean being cheap or sacrificing quality. Instead, it's about being intentional with your spending and prioritizing the things that truly matter to you. For example, I love to travel, so instead of booking the cheapest possible flights and accommodations, I spend time researching and finding the best deals on high-quality travel experiences that fit within my budget.

It's also important to let go of the idea that material possessions equate to happiness. While it can be tempting to buy things in order to feel better or to impress others, the truth is that material possessions only provide temporary satisfaction. Instead, I find fulfillment in experiences and relationships, which bring lasting happiness and memories.

Finally, a frugal mindset involves being mindful of your resources and the impact that your choices have on the world around you. This means reducing waste, using resources wisely, and making choices that align with your values. For example, I choose to buy locally grown produce and support small businesses, which not only reduces my carbon footprint but also helps to support my local community.

In conclusion, finding the right mindset is essential for living a frugal life. It involves shifting your focus from what you lack to what you have, prioritizing the things that truly matter to you, finding joy in simple pleasures, and being mindful of your impact on the world. By developing a frugal mindset, you can find financial freedom, fulfillment, and a deeper appreciation for the abundance in your life.

The Secret to Frugal Grocery Shopping

When it comes to frugalism, one of the most important areas to focus on is grocery shopping. After all, food is a necessity, and it's also one of the biggest expenses for most households. However, with a few simple strategies, it's possible to save money on groceries while still eating well.

One of the key secrets to frugal grocery shopping is to plan ahead. This means making a list of what you need before you go to the store and sticking to it. It also means taking the time to look at sales flyers and coupons to find the best deals. For example, if you know that chicken breasts are on sale this week, plan your meals around that and stock up.

Another important strategy is to buy in bulk. This doesn't mean you have to go to a warehouse store and buy a year's supply of toilet paper, but it does mean that you should consider buying larger quantities of items that you use regularly. For example, if you eat oatmeal every morning, buying a large container of oats is likely more cost-effective than buying individual packets.

It's also important to be mindful of where you shop. While it can be tempting to do all of your shopping at one store for convenience, different stores often have different prices and sales. For example, I find that my local grocery store has the best prices on produce, but the nearby farmer's market has great deals on meat and dairy.

When it comes to the actual shopping trip, there are a few tricks that can help you save money. First, shop with a full stomach to avoid impulse purchases. Second, try to stick to the perimeter of the store, where the fresh produce, meat, and dairy are located, rather than the center aisles where the processed and packaged foods are located. Finally, consider buying store brands rather than name brands. In many cases, the quality is the same, but the price is lower.

One personal example of how I save money on groceries is by meal planning. At the beginning of the week, I sit down and plan out what meals I'll be making for the week, based on what I already have in my pantry and what's on sale at the store. I make a list of all the ingredients I'll need and then stick to that list when I go shopping. By doing this, I'm able to avoid last-minute takeout orders and wasted food, which helps me save money in the long run.

In conclusion, frugal grocery shopping is all about planning ahead, buying in bulk, being mindful of where you shop, and making smart choices in the store. By following these strategies, you can save money on your grocery bill while still eating well and enjoying delicious meals.

Meal Planning on a Tight Budget

One of the most effective ways to save money on food is through meal planning. By planning out your meals in advance, you can shop strategically, avoid last-minute takeout orders, and reduce food waste. However, when you're on a tight budget, meal planning can seem like a daunting task. But fear not, there are plenty of ways to plan meals on a budget without sacrificing taste or nutrition.

The first step in meal planning on a tight budget is to take stock of what you already have in your pantry and fridge. This will help you to avoid buying ingredients that you don't need and to use up items that are close to their expiration date. Once you know what you have, you can start to plan your meals for the week.

When planning meals on a budget, it's important to focus on affordable, nutrient-dense foods. This means incorporating plenty of fruits, vegetables, whole grains, and lean protein sources into your meals. It's also important to be mindful of portion sizes and to avoid wasting food. Leftovers can be repurposed for lunch the next day or frozen for future meals.

Another key strategy is to buy ingredients in bulk. This can be especially cost-effective for staples like grains, beans, and nuts. By buying in bulk, you can save money and ensure that you always have these ingredients on hand when you need them.

One personal example of how I plan meals on a budget is by using the "cook once, eat twice" approach. For example, if I'm making a pot of chili, I'll make a double batch and freeze half for later. This not only saves money on ingredients but also saves time on meal prep in the future.

Another personal strategy is to use seasonal produce. In-season produce is often less expensive and tastes better than out-of-season produce that has to be shipped from far away. I also try to shop at local farmer's markets, where I can often find affordable, fresh produce.

When it comes to the actual meal planning process, I find it helpful to plan meals around ingredients that are on sale that week. I also try to plan meals that use similar ingredients, so that I can buy in bulk and use ingredients in multiple meals.

In conclusion, meal planning on a tight budget can be challenging, but it's not impossible. By focusing on affordable, nutrient-dense ingredients, buying in bulk, and being mindful of food waste, you can save money on your grocery bill and still enjoy delicious and nutritious meals. With a little bit of planning and creativity, meal planning on a tight budget can become a fun and rewarding part of your frugal lifestyle.

Reducing Waste and Saving Money

In a world where waste is so prevalent, it's important to make an effort to reduce it whenever possible. Not only is this good for the environment, but it can also save you money in the long run. Here are some tips and personal examples for reducing waste and saving money in your daily life.

One of the easiest ways to reduce waste is to bring your own reusable bags when shopping. This can include reusable grocery bags, produce bags, and even shopping bags for other types of stores. By using reusable bags, you can avoid using single-use plastic bags that end up in landfills or oceans.

Another way to reduce waste is to use reusable containers for food storage. Instead of using disposable plastic bags or containers, opt for reusable containers made of glass or metal. These can be used over and over again, and can help reduce the amount of waste you generate.

When it comes to food waste, meal planning is an important strategy. By planning your meals in advance and buying only what you need, you can reduce the amount of food that goes to waste. This can save you money on your grocery bill and reduce the amount of food that ends up in landfills.

Another way to reduce food waste is to compost. Composting is a natural process that breaks down organic materials like food scraps and yard waste into nutrient-rich soil. By composting, you can reduce the amount of waste that goes into landfills and create your own fertilizer for your garden or houseplants. I personally started composting after I learned about the benefits of it and how easy it is to do. Now, I feel good knowing that I'm not throwing away food scraps and other organic waste, and instead using them to create something useful.

In addition to reducing waste in your home, there are other ways to reduce waste and save money when you're out and about. For example, bringing your own reusable water bottle can help you avoid buying bottled water, which not only reduces waste but also saves you money in the long run. The same goes for bringing your own coffee cup when you go to a coffee shop. Another way to reduce waste is to avoid single-use plastic utensils and straws when eating out. Instead, bring your own reusable utensils and straws made of bamboo or metal. By doing so, you can help reduce the amount of plastic waste that ends up in landfills and oceans.

Finally, when it comes to reducing waste and saving money, it's important to think about the long-term impact of your purchases. Instead of buying cheap, disposable items that will need to be replaced frequently, invest in high-quality, durable items that will last a long time. This may mean spending a bit more money upfront, but it can save you money in the long run by avoiding frequent replacements and reducing waste.

In conclusion, there are many ways to reduce waste and save money in your daily life. By making simple changes to your shopping and lifestyle habits, you can make a positive impact on the environment and your finances. The key is to start small and take one step at a time towards a more frugal and sustainable lifestyle.

Simple DIY Hacks to Save Money

In a world where everything seems to be getting more expensive, it's important to find ways to save money wherever possible. One great way to do this is through simple do-it-yourself (DIY) hacks that can save you money on everyday items. Here are some of my personal favorite DIY hacks for saving money.

One of the simplest DIY hacks for saving money is to make your own cleaning products. Many store-bought cleaning products are filled with chemicals and can be expensive, but you can easily make your own using simple ingredients like vinegar, baking soda, and lemon juice. Not only are these ingredients inexpensive, but they're also eco-friendly and non-toxic.

Another way to save money through DIY is to make your own personal care products. Many beauty and personal care products are also filled with chemicals and can be expensive, but you can make your own using natural ingredients like coconut oil, essential oils, and beeswax. Not only are these ingredients less expensive than store-bought products, but they're also better for your skin and hair.

When it comes to home décor, there are many DIY hacks that can save you money. For example, instead of buying expensive art for your walls, you can create your own using materials like canvas, paint, and stencils. You can also repurpose items you already have in your home, like old jars or bottles, to create unique and inexpensive décor.

Another great way to save money through DIY is to make your own clothing and accessories. Whether it's sewing a new outfit, knitting a scarf, or making jewelry, there are endless possibilities for creating your own fashion items. Not only can this save you money on buying new clothes and accessories, but it can also be a fun and creative hobby.

In addition to these personal examples, there are many other simple DIY hacks that can save you money in your daily life. For example, you can make your own laundry detergent, create your own storage solutions using items you already have, or even build your own furniture using repurposed materials.

In conclusion, there are many simple and creative DIY hacks that can save you money in your daily life. By taking the time to make your own cleaning products, personal care items, home décor, clothing, and accessories, you can save money while also being more environmentally friendly and adding a personal touch to your everyday items. The key is to be creative, resourceful, and willing to try new things.

The Beauty of Thrift Store Finds

In a world where fast fashion dominates, it can be easy to forget about the beauty of thrift store finds. However, shopping at thrift stores can be a great way to save money while also discovering unique and one-of-a-kind pieces. Here are some of my personal experiences and tips for shopping at thrift stores.

One of the best things about thrift stores is the variety of items available. You can find anything from clothing and accessories to home décor and furniture, often at a fraction of the cost of buying new. Plus, you never know what treasures you might stumble upon! Some of my favorite thrift store finds include vintage dresses, unique jewelry pieces, and quirky home décor items.

Another great thing about shopping at thrift stores is the sustainability factor. By buying secondhand items, you're reducing the amount of waste that goes into landfills and supporting a more circular economy. It's also a great way to find items that may be out of production or hard to find in stores, making your finds even more special.

When shopping at thrift stores, it's important to have an open mind and be willing to search through the racks. You may have to sift through some less desirable items, but the payoff is worth it when you find that perfect piece. It's also important to keep in mind that sizing and quality can vary, so be sure to inspect items carefully before purchasing.

One of my personal favorite thrift store finds was a vintage leather jacket that I scored for a fraction of its original price. It's a piece that I've worn for years and always receive compliments on. I've also found unique home décor items, like a set of vintage brass candlesticks, that add character to my living space.

In addition to personal finds, there are many other reasons to love thrift stores. For example, many thrift stores support charitable causes, so your purchases are also supporting a good cause. Plus, you can often find designer items at a fraction of their original cost, making high-end fashion more accessible.

In conclusion, shopping at thrift stores is a great way to save money while also discovering unique and one-of-a-kind pieces. With an open mind and a willingness to search through the racks, you can find anything from vintage clothing to quirky home décor items. Not only are thrift store finds more sustainable, but they also support charitable causes and make high-end fashion more accessible. So next time you're in the market for something new, consider taking a trip to your local thrift store and seeing what treasures you can uncover.

Prioritizing Experiences over Things

As humans, we tend to accumulate things over time. We buy clothes, furniture, gadgets, and countless other items that we think we need. However, as we amass more and more possessions, we often lose sight of what truly brings us happiness: experiences. In this chapter, I will discuss the importance of prioritizing experiences over things and share some personal examples.

One of the main reasons why experiences are more valuable than things is because they have a lasting impact on our happiness. While the initial thrill of buying a new possession might be exciting, it eventually fades away. In contrast, the memories and feelings associated with experiences stay with us forever. For example, I vividly remember the time I went on a road trip with my friends, exploring different parts of the country and making memories that I will cherish for a lifetime. On the other hand, I can barely remember the last time I bought a new piece of clothing.

Another reason why experiences are more important than things is that they help us connect with others. When we share experiences with friends and family, we create deeper connections and strengthen our relationships. This is because experiences give us something to bond over and reminisce about in the future. For example, I have fond memories of hiking in the mountains with my family and the conversations we had along the way. Those experiences helped us build stronger relationships with each other.

There are many ways to prioritize experiences over things in our daily lives. For example, instead of buying new clothes or gadgets, we can spend our money on experiences like travel, concerts, or dining out with friends. We can also make a conscious effort to spend more time with the people we care about and focus on creating meaningful memories together.

One personal example of prioritizing experiences over things in my life is my decision to take a gap year after finishing university. Instead of jumping right into a career, I decided to travel and explore the world. During that year, I visited many different countries, met new people, and had experiences that changed my perspective on life. Looking back, I don't regret that decision at all. The memories and lessons I learned during that time have stayed with me and continue to shape my life today.

In conclusion, while possessions can provide us with temporary pleasure, experiences are much more valuable in the long run. They create lasting memories, help us connect with others, and bring us true happiness. By prioritizing experiences over things, we can lead a more fulfilling life and create meaningful connections with the people around us. So the next time you're considering buying something new, ask yourself if that purchase will truly make you happy, or if you could use that money to create a meaningful experience instead.

How to Travel on a Shoestring Budget

Traveling is a wonderful experience that allows us to explore new places, learn about different cultures, and make unforgettable memories. However, the cost of travel can often be a barrier for many people. In this chapter, I will discuss how to travel on a shoestring budget and share some personal examples.

The first step to traveling on a budget is to plan ahead. Research your destination, including the cost of transportation, accommodations, and food. Look for deals and discounts on flights, hotels, and activities. Many websites and apps offer great deals for budget travelers.

Another way to save money while traveling is to be flexible with your travel dates. Traveling during the off-season or mid-week can often result in lower prices for flights, accommodations, and activities. In addition, consider staying in budget-friendly accommodations like hostels, guesthouses, or Airbnb rentals instead of luxury hotels.

When it comes to food, eating like a local can often be more budget-friendly than dining at tourist hotspots. Look for street food vendors or local markets to get a taste of the local cuisine without breaking the bank. You can also save money on food by packing snacks or bringing your own water bottle to refill.

One of my personal examples of traveling on a shoestring budget was when I visited Thailand a few years ago. I traveled during the off-season and booked my flights and accommodations well in advance. I stayed in budget-friendly guesthouses and hostels and ate at local markets and street food vendors. I also took advantage of free activities like hiking and visiting temples, as well as low-cost activities like renting a scooter to explore the island.

Another way to save money while traveling is to use public transportation instead of taxis or private transportation. Many cities have affordable public transportation options like buses, trains, or subways. Walking or biking is also a great way to explore a new city while staying active and saving money.

Lastly, consider taking advantage of free or low-cost activities like visiting museums, parks, or historic sites. Many cities offer free walking tours or have events and festivals throughout the year that are open to the public.

In conclusion, traveling on a shoestring budget requires careful planning, flexibility, and a willingness to embrace the local culture. By being smart with your spending, you can experience the beauty and wonder of travel without breaking the bank. So pack your bags, grab your guidebook, and get ready to embark on an affordable adventure!

Staying Fashionable on a Frugal Budget

Staying fashionable can be a challenge, especially when you're on a tight budget. However, with a little creativity and resourcefulness, it's possible to look stylish and put-together without breaking the bank. In this chapter, I will share some tips and personal examples for staying fashionable on a frugal budget.

The first step to staying fashionable on a budget is to assess your wardrobe and identify the items you really need. Think about your personal style and the occasions you need to dress for. Consider investing in versatile, classic pieces like a well-fitting pair of jeans, a tailored blazer, and a little black dress.

When it comes to shopping for clothes, there are plenty of affordable options out there. Consider shopping at thrift stores, consignment shops, and online marketplaces. You can often find high-quality, stylish clothing for a fraction of the retail price.

Another way to save money on clothes is to shop end-of-season sales or clearance racks. This is a great way to score designer clothing at a discount. You can also sign up for email newsletters or follow your favorite brands on social media to stay updated on sales and promotions.

If you're handy with a sewing machine, consider upcycling or repurposing old clothing to create new, fashionable pieces. You can also swap clothes with friends or participate in clothing swaps in your community.

One of my personal examples of staying fashionable on a frugal budget was when I needed a dress for a formal event. Instead of buying a new dress, I borrowed one from a friend and accessorized it with a statement necklace and earrings. I felt confident and stylish without spending a dime.

Accessories can also help elevate your look and add a personal touch to your outfit. Consider investing in statement pieces like a colorful scarf, a bold statement necklace, or a classic leather bag. These pieces can be mixed and matched with different outfits to create a variety of looks.

Lastly, take care of your clothes to make them last longer. Follow care instructions on the labels and use a clothesline or drying rack instead of a dryer to avoid shrinkage or damage. You can also invest in a good quality steamer or iron to keep your clothes looking fresh and crisp.

In conclusion, staying fashionable on a frugal budget requires a mix of creativity, resourcefulness, and smart shopping. By focusing on versatile, classic pieces and taking advantage of affordable options like thrift stores and end-of-season sales, you can look stylish and put-together without spending a lot of money. So go ahead and experiment with your personal style, and don't be afraid to think outside the box!

The Importance of Saving for a Rainy Day

In life, there are unexpected moments that can completely disrupt our financial stability. Whether it's a sudden job loss, a medical emergency, or a car accident, we never know when we may need a rainy day fund to get us through tough times. This is why it's important to make saving a priority in our lives, and to always have a financial safety net to fall back on.

When I first started my frugal journey, I was living paycheck to paycheck and had no savings to speak of. It wasn't until I experienced a medical emergency that left me with a hefty hospital bill that I realized the importance of having a rainy day fund. I knew I needed to make saving a priority if I wanted to be financially secure and prepared for any unexpected expenses.

To start building my rainy day fund, I first had to make a budget that allowed me to set aside money each month. I started by setting a realistic savings goal and created a separate savings account that was only for emergency expenses. This helped me keep my savings separate from my regular spending money, and I was less likely to dip into it for non-essential expenses.

I also made sure to cut back on unnecessary expenses, so I could put more money towards my savings. This meant saying no to eating out, canceling subscriptions I didn't need, and finding ways to reduce my monthly bills. It wasn't always easy, but I knew that each dollar I saved would bring me one step closer to my goal of financial security.

As I continued to save, I started to feel a sense of relief knowing that I had a safety net in case of emergencies. It allowed me to breathe easier, knowing that I had some financial cushion to fall back on. I no longer had to worry about how I would pay for unexpected expenses, and I could focus on other aspects of my life without the constant stress of financial uncertainty.

In the end, having a rainy day fund was one of the best financial decisions I ever made. It gave me peace of mind, allowed me to handle unexpected expenses with ease, and provided a solid foundation for building a more stable financial future. I learned that it's never too late to start saving, and even small amounts can add up over time. By making saving a priority and embracing a frugal lifestyle, anyone can achieve financial security and peace of mind.

Frugal Ways to Celebrate Special Occasions

As the year rolls on, we all encounter special occasions, whether it be birthdays, anniversaries, or holidays. However, many people believe that celebrating these events means spending a lot of money. Fortunately, there are many ways to make these special moments memorable without breaking the bank.

One way to celebrate a special occasion on a frugal budget is to plan ahead. It's important to make a list of the people you want to celebrate with and decide on the type of celebration you want to have. Do you want a big party, a small gathering, or a special activity? Once you have an idea in mind, it's time to start making plans.

For instance, when I celebrated my daughter's birthday, I decided to have a simple party at home. Instead of ordering a pricey cake, I baked a cake myself, and we made homemade decorations with construction paper and markers. We also had a few fun games that the kids enjoyed playing, and I made goodie bags for each of them to take home. It was a memorable day, and we didn't have to spend a lot of money to make it special.

Another way to celebrate a special occasion on a frugal budget is to get creative with gifts. Rather than buying an expensive present, you can make something meaningful instead. For example, if you're celebrating a wedding anniversary, you could make a scrapbook of all your favorite memories together. Or if you're celebrating a child's birthday, you could create a personalized coloring book or a photo album of their favorite moments from the past year.

When my husband and I celebrated our anniversary, we decided to have a picnic in the park instead of going out to a fancy restaurant. We made sandwiches and snacks at home and packed them in a basket, along with a bottle of wine. We spent the day enjoying the sunshine and each other's company, and it was one of the most memorable anniversaries we've had.

You can also celebrate special occasions by doing something fun that doesn't require a lot of money. For example, you could have a movie night with friends, host a potluck dinner, or have a game night. These activities are fun and don't cost a lot of money.

Lastly, it's important to remember that the people you're celebrating with are what make the occasion special, not the amount of money you spend. So don't be afraid to get creative and find ways to celebrate special occasions on a frugal budget. With a little planning and creativity, you can make these moments unforgettable without breaking the bank.

Tips for Hosting a Frugal Party

As the holiday season approaches, the urge to throw a lavish party can be strong. However, for those on a tight budget, the thought of spending a small fortune on one event can be overwhelming. Fear not, dear readers, for I am here to offer some tips on how to host a fabulous party without breaking the bank.

First and foremost, it is important to set a budget for your party. This will help guide your decisions on everything from the guest list to the menu. Once you have a budget in mind, it's time to start planning.

One frugal way to save money is to make your own invitations. You can find countless templates online and print them out on cardstock. This will not only save you money but also add a personal touch to your invitations.

When it comes to the menu, consider serving items that can be made in bulk and in advance. This will not only save you time but also money. For example, a large pot of chili or a big batch of pasta salad can be filling and satisfying for your guests.

Another tip is to avoid buying expensive decorations. Instead, consider using items you already have around your home. Candles, flowers, and simple tablecloths can all add a touch of elegance to your party without breaking the bank.

If you're planning on serving alcohol, consider making a signature cocktail instead of offering a full bar. This will not only save you money, but it will also add a fun and unique touch to your party.

When it comes to entertainment, consider hosting a game night or a movie night. These types of activities are fun and require minimal preparation. If you do want to hire a performer, consider looking for up-and-coming artists who may offer their services at a lower rate.

Finally, don't be afraid to ask for help from your guests. You can ask them to bring a dish to share or help with setting up and cleaning up. Most people are happy to contribute and will be honored to be a part of your special occasion.

Remember, the most important part of any party is spending time with the people you love. By following these tips, you can create a memorable event without breaking the bank.

Understanding Your Spending Triggers

It's easy to overspend and not even realize it. Sometimes, it feels like our money just disappears, and we can't figure out where it went. This is why it's important to understand our spending triggers.

A spending trigger is something that causes us to spend money impulsively or unnecessarily. It could be a certain emotion, like stress or boredom, that causes us to go shopping or buy something we don't need. It could also be a certain situation, like going out to eat with friends or walking by a store that's having a sale.

For me, one of my biggest spending triggers used to be stress. Whenever I had a stressful day at work or school, I would go shopping to make myself feel better. I didn't even realize I was doing it until I looked at my credit card statement and saw how much I had spent on things I didn't need.

Once you identify your spending triggers, you can take steps to avoid them. For example, if stress is a trigger for you, find other ways to cope with stress, like going for a walk or taking a relaxing bath. If going out to eat with friends is a trigger, suggest alternative activities like a picnic or a game night at home.

It's also important to be mindful of your spending triggers when making purchases. Before making a purchase, ask yourself if it's something you really need or if it's just a impulse buy. You can also try setting a waiting period before making a purchase. If you still want the item after a week or two, then it's probably something you really want and will use.

Another way to avoid spending triggers is to have a budget and stick to it. By setting limits on your spending, you can avoid overspending and impulse buying. This can also help you prioritize your spending on the things that are important to you.

Understanding your spending triggers takes time and practice, but it can have a big impact on your finances. By identifying your triggers and taking steps to avoid them, you can make better financial decisions and achieve your goals more quickly.

Dealing with Social Pressure to Spend

As humans, we are social creatures. We seek validation and approval from our peers, and often, this can lead to social pressure to spend. Whether it's feeling the need to keep up with friends' spending habits or conforming to societal expectations of what it means to be successful, the pressure to spend can be intense.

In order to maintain a frugal lifestyle, it's important to learn how to deal with this pressure in a healthy way. This chapter will explore the various ways in which social pressure to spend can manifest, and provide tips on how to navigate these situations without compromising your financial goals.

One of the most common forms of social pressure to spend is through peer influence. We often feel compelled to keep up with our friends' lifestyles, even if it means spending money we don't have. For example, if your friend group loves going out to expensive restaurants every weekend, you might feel left out if you can't afford to join them. However, it's important to remember that your financial health should always come first. It's okay to decline invitations if they don't fit within your budget, or suggest alternative, less expensive activities that everyone can enjoy.

Another form of social pressure to spend comes from societal expectations. We are often bombarded with images of what it means to be successful, and these images are usually tied to material possessions. It's important to remember that true success and happiness cannot be measured by the things we own. Living a frugal lifestyle means prioritizing experiences and relationships over material possessions. This can be a difficult mindset shift, but one that is necessary for long-term financial health.

One personal example of dealing with social pressure to spend comes from my university days. As a student, it was common for my peers to spend a lot of money on alcohol and partying. However, I knew that this was not a sustainable or healthy way to live. I had to learn how to say no to certain activities and create my own, less expensive ways of having fun. This often meant finding free events or activities around the city, or hosting potluck dinners with friends instead of going out to restaurants.

Another example comes from my professional life. When I started my first job, I felt the need to dress a certain way and have all the latest gadgets in order to fit in with my colleagues. However, I quickly realized that this was not sustainable for my budget. Instead, I focused on developing my skills and building strong relationships with my colleagues, which ultimately led to more opportunities for growth and advancement.

In conclusion, dealing with social pressure to spend can be a challenge, but it's an important part of maintaining a frugal lifestyle. By prioritizing your financial health, learning to say no, and shifting your mindset away from material possessions, you can create a fulfilling and sustainable life that is true to your values. Remember, true success and happiness cannot be bought with money.

Setting Realistic Financial Goals

As a frugalist, setting realistic financial goals is a crucial part of your journey to achieving financial freedom. Without goals, it can be easy to lose sight of why you're making sacrifices and living a more modest lifestyle. In this chapter, we'll explore the importance of setting financial goals, how to set them, and how to stick to them.

The Importance of Setting Financial Goals

Setting financial goals helps you stay focused on what you want to achieve. It gives you a clear direction and purpose, and helps you make better decisions about how to use your money. Goals can be short-term or long-term, and they should be specific, measurable, attainable, relevant, and time-bound. These criteria are commonly referred to as SMART goals.

For example, a short-term SMART goal could be to save $500 in three months. A long-term SMART goal could be to save $10,000 for a down payment on a house in two years. By setting specific and measurable goals, you'll be able to track your progress and make adjustments as needed.

How to Set Realistic Financial Goals

To set realistic financial goals, start by identifying your priorities. Do you want to pay off debt, save for retirement, or save for a down payment on a house? Once you have a clear idea of what you want to achieve, you can start setting SMART goals.

It's important to be realistic when setting your goals. If you set goals that are too ambitious, you may become discouraged and give up. On the other hand, if your goals are too easy, you may not feel motivated to work towards them.

To set realistic goals, take a look at your current financial situation. How much money do you have coming in each month? How much are you spending? Are there any areas where you can cut back on expenses? Use this information to set goals that are challenging but achievable.

For example, if you're currently saving $50 a month, a goal of saving $500 a month may not be realistic. Instead, set a goal of saving $75 or $100 a month and work your way up from there.

How to Stick to Your Goals

Once you've set your financial goals, it's important to stay motivated and focused. One way to do this is to break your goals down into smaller milestones. For example, if your goal is to save $5,000 in a year, set a milestone of saving $1,000 every three months. This will help you stay on track and feel a sense of accomplishment along the way.

It's also important to track your progress regularly. This can be as simple as keeping a spreadsheet or using a budgeting app to monitor your spending and savings. Seeing your progress in black and white can be very motivating and help you stay on track.

Finally, don't be afraid to make adjustments to your goals as needed. Life is unpredictable, and your financial situation may change unexpectedly. If you need to adjust your goals, that's okay. The most important thing is to stay focused on your long-term vision of financial freedom.

When I first started my frugal journey, I set a goal to pay off my credit card debt within a year. I had accumulated over $5,000 in credit card debt and was struggling to make the minimum payments. I set a SMART goal to pay off my debt by making extra payments every month and cutting back on unnecessary expenses.

To stay motivated, I broke my goal down into smaller milestones. Every time I paid off $500 of my debt, I rewarded myself with a small treat like a movie or a nice dinner. Tracking my progress on a spreadsheet helped me see how far I had come and kept me focused on my goal.

The Benefits of a Frugal Mindset

As I've journeyed through the world of frugalism, I've come to realize that there are many benefits to living a life of simplicity and financial responsibility. In this chapter, I'll explore some of the most significant benefits I've experienced in my own life.

First and foremost, adopting a frugal mindset has allowed me to live a more intentional and fulfilling life. Instead of spending money on things that don't truly bring me joy, I'm able to invest in experiences that matter to me, like traveling or pursuing hobbies I'm passionate about. This has led to a greater sense of purpose and satisfaction in my daily life.

In addition, living frugally has given me a greater sense of control over my finances. By budgeting and tracking my spending, I'm able to make informed decisions about how to use my money and plan for the future. This has helped me feel more secure and less stressed about money-related issues.

Another benefit of frugal living is the positive impact it can have on the environment. By consuming less and recycling more, I'm doing my part to reduce waste and conserve resources. This has led to a greater sense of connection to the planet and a desire to live in harmony with it.

Living frugally has also helped me build a sense of community and connection with others. By participating in shared activities that don't require a lot of money, like potluck dinners or outdoor activities, I've been able to build relationships with people who share my values and interests. This has led to a sense of belonging and a support system that I can rely on.

Finally, living frugally has allowed me to save money and build a strong financial foundation for the future. By prioritizing saving and investing, I'm setting myself up for long-term success and security. This has given me a greater sense of peace of mind and a feeling of being in control of my financial future.

In conclusion, adopting a frugal mindset can have many benefits beyond just saving money. It can lead to a more intentional and fulfilling life, a greater sense of control over finances, a positive impact on the environment, a sense of community and connection with others, and a strong financial foundation for the future. I've found that these benefits have made the effort of living frugally well worth it, and I encourage anyone who is interested to explore this way of life for themselves.

Frugal Habits for a Sustainable Future

In a world where resources are becoming scarce and the environment is suffering, it is more important than ever to adopt frugal habits that are sustainable for the future. Not only do these habits help preserve the planet, but they also help you save money in the long run.

One of the most effective ways to live sustainably is to reduce your use of plastic. Single-use plastic products such as straws, water bottles, and shopping bags can take hundreds of years to decompose, and often end up in the ocean, harming wildlife and the environment. By investing in reusable products, such as metal or glass straws, refillable water bottles, and cloth bags, you can significantly reduce your carbon footprint while saving money.

Another important habit to adopt is to reduce food waste. In the United States alone, nearly 40% of all food produced goes to waste. This not only wastes resources, but it also wastes your hard-earned money. By planning meals ahead of time, shopping smart, and using up leftovers, you can significantly reduce the amount of food you throw away. Composting is also a great way to use up food scraps and create nutrient-rich soil for your garden or plants.

Gardening is another great way to live sustainably and save money. Growing your own vegetables and fruits can be a fun and rewarding experience, and it helps reduce your reliance on store-bought produce that may have been shipped long distances. If you don't have access to a garden, consider growing plants in containers or window boxes. Even growing herbs can save you money on your grocery bill and reduce your environmental impact.

It's also important to reduce your energy usage and make your home more energy-efficient. Small changes, such as turning off lights when leaving a room, using LED light bulbs, and unplugging electronics when not in use, can add up to significant savings on your energy bill. Installing a programmable thermostat can also help you save money by automatically adjusting the temperature in your home when you're away.

When it comes to transportation, there are many frugal and sustainable options available. Walking or biking to your destination is not only great exercise, but it also reduces your carbon footprint and saves money on gas and car maintenance. If you need to travel further, consider using public transportation, carpooling, or investing in a fuel-efficient vehicle.

By adopting these frugal and sustainable habits, you can make a positive impact on the environment while also saving money. It's important to remember that every small action makes a difference, and by working together, we can create a brighter and more sustainable future for generations to come.

Personally, I've adopted many of these habits in my own life. I always carry a reusable water bottle and cloth bags with me, and I've started growing herbs in my kitchen. I also make a conscious effort to turn off lights and unplug electronics when not in use, and I've started using a programmable thermostat. These small changes have helped me save money and reduce my environmental impact, and I feel good knowing that I'm doing my part to create a more sustainable future.

Overcoming the Fear of Missing Out

As we navigate through the world, it's easy to get caught up in the trap of comparison and fear of missing out, or FOMO for short. It's a phenomenon that has become more and more prevalent in recent years, particularly with the rise of social media. We're constantly bombarded with images and updates from others' lives, and it's easy to start feeling like we're not doing enough or that we're missing out on something.

But the truth is, living a frugal lifestyle doesn't mean missing out on anything. In fact, it can actually lead to a more fulfilling life. When you learn to let go of the fear of missing out, you can start living in the present moment and appreciating what you have, rather than always striving for something more.

One of the first steps to overcoming the fear of missing out is to recognize that it's a common feeling, and that it's okay to feel that way. It's natural to want to be part of a group or experience what others are experiencing. However, it's important to keep in mind that not everything that's popular or trendy is necessarily good for us or aligned with our values.

Another way to overcome FOMO is to focus on gratitude. Take time to appreciate what you already have in your life, and the experiences and opportunities that have brought you to where you are today. When you shift your focus to gratitude, you can start to see that what you have is already enough, and you don't need to constantly seek out more.

It's also important to set priorities for your life, and stick to them. When you have a clear understanding of what's important to you, it becomes easier to say no to things that don't align with those values. For example, if you're prioritizing saving for a house or paying off debt, you might choose to skip a weekend trip with friends in favor of a more affordable activity, or to stay home altogether.

Personal examples of how I have overcome the fear of missing out in my own life include being intentional about my social media use. I limit my time on these platforms, and when I do use them, I'm mindful of how they make me feel. I also prioritize experiences and activities that align with my values, such as spending time in nature or with loved ones, rather than trying to keep up with the latest trends.

In conclusion, the fear of missing out is a real feeling that many of us experience, but it doesn't have to control our lives. By focusing on gratitude, setting priorities, and being intentional about our choices, we can overcome this fear and live a more fulfilling, frugal life.

Navigating the Pitfalls of Credit Cards

Credit cards can be a useful tool for building credit, earning rewards, and providing financial flexibility. However, they can also be a source of temptation and lead to financial ruin if not used responsibly. In this chapter, we will explore the pitfalls of credit cards and how to navigate them with a frugal mindset.

First and foremost, it is important to understand that credit cards are not free money. Any purchases made with a credit card will need to be paid back with interest, which can quickly add up and become unmanageable. Therefore, it is essential to only use credit cards for purchases that can be paid off in full each month.

One common pitfall of credit cards is overspending. It can be easy to fall into the trap of thinking that because you have a credit card, you have unlimited funds. However, it is important to set a budget for yourself and stick to it. Only use your credit card for expenses that are within your budget, and do not be tempted to overspend just because you have the option to do so.

Another pitfall of credit cards is not fully understanding the terms and conditions. It is important to read the fine print and understand the interest rate, fees, and any other charges associated with your credit card. Make sure you understand the due dates and minimum payments required, as missing a payment can lead to late fees and damage to your credit score.

Credit card rewards can be a great way to save money or earn perks, but they can also be a trap. Do not be tempted to overspend just to earn rewards, as the interest and fees will quickly negate any benefits. Additionally, make sure to choose a credit card with rewards that are relevant to your lifestyle, as some rewards may not be useful or valuable to you.

One of the biggest pitfalls of credit cards is not paying off the balance in full each month. Carrying a balance on a credit card can lead to high interest charges, which can quickly snowball into unmanageable debt. If you are unable to pay off your credit card balance in full each month, it is best to avoid using credit cards altogether until you are able to do so.

Lastly, it is important to monitor your credit score and report regularly. Credit card debt and missed payments can have a negative impact on your credit score, which can make it more difficult to obtain loans or credit in the future. By monitoring your credit score and report, you can catch any errors or fraudulent activity early and take steps to correct them.

In conclusion, credit cards can be a useful tool for managing your finances, but they can also be a source of temptation and lead to financial ruin if not used responsibly. By understanding the pitfalls of credit cards and developing a frugal mindset, you can use credit cards to your advantage and avoid falling into debt. Remember to set a budget, read the fine print, choose rewards wisely, pay off your balance in full each month, and monitor your credit score and report. With these strategies in mind, you can navigate the pitfalls of credit cards and achieve financial stability.

Finding Support in Your Frugal Journey

As you begin your frugal journey, you may feel alone or isolated, especially if your friends and family don't share your values. However, there are many resources available to help you stay on track and find the support you need to succeed.

One of the best places to start is online. There are countless frugal living blogs, social media groups, and forums that can provide you with advice, tips, and support. You can connect with like-minded people who share your goals and struggles, and learn from their experiences.

Additionally, there are many apps available that can help you manage your finances, set goals, and track your progress. These apps can make it easier to stay on top of your budget and savings goals, and can also help you identify areas where you can cut back.

You may also want to consider attending local events or meetings. Many cities have frugal living groups, where you can meet others who are also trying to save money and live a more sustainable lifestyle. These groups may organize events such as potlucks, swap meets, or group outings, providing an opportunity to connect with others in person.

Another option is to seek out a mentor or accountability partner. This could be someone who has more experience with frugal living, or someone who is also starting out and wants to work together to stay motivated and accountable.

Lastly, don't forget to seek support from those closest to you, such as family and friends. While they may not share your frugal values, they can still support you by encouraging your efforts and respecting your choices.

When I first started my frugal journey, I felt overwhelmed and unsure of myself. However, I found a lot of support online, through frugal living blogs and social media groups. I was inspired by the stories of others who had achieved financial freedom and a simpler, more fulfilling lifestyle through frugality.

I also attended a local frugal living group, which provided an opportunity to connect with others in my community who were pursuing a similar path. Through this group, I made several friends who provided me with ongoing support and encouragement.

Lastly, I found a mentor who had been living a frugal lifestyle for many years. She was able to provide me with advice and guidance as I navigated the challenges of cutting back and saving money. Her support was invaluable in helping me stay on track and motivated.

Maintaining a Positive Outlook on Frugal Living

It's easy to get bogged down in the day-to-day details of living a frugal lifestyle. Focusing on what you can't do or can't buy can take a toll on your mental health and overall happiness. But it doesn't have to be that way. In fact, embracing a frugal lifestyle can lead to a more fulfilling life in the long run. It's all about maintaining a positive outlook and focusing on the benefits of living a frugal life.

One way to maintain a positive outlook is to focus on what you can do instead of what you can't. For example, instead of focusing on all the things you can't buy, focus on the experiences you can have. Instead of buying a new outfit, plan a fun day trip with friends or family. You'll create memories that will last much longer than any material possession.

Another way to maintain a positive outlook is to practice gratitude. Be thankful for what you have instead of focusing on what you don't have. Take a moment each day to reflect on the things in your life that you're grateful for, whether it's your health, your family, your job, or your home. It's easy to take these things for granted, but practicing gratitude can help you stay positive and appreciative of what you have.

It's also important to remember that living a frugal lifestyle doesn't mean living a deprived lifestyle. There are plenty of ways to enjoy life without breaking the bank. Look for free or low-cost activities in your area, such as hiking, visiting a museum, or attending a community event. You'll be surprised at how many opportunities there are to have fun without spending a lot of money.

And don't forget to celebrate your successes along the way. When you achieve a financial goal or make a smart purchase, take a moment to acknowledge and celebrate it. This will help you stay motivated and positive about your frugal lifestyle.

Finally, surround yourself with positive influences. Connect with like-minded people who share your values and goals. This could mean joining a frugal living group or attending events focused on sustainable living. You'll find a supportive community that can help you stay positive and motivated.

In my own life, I've found that maintaining a positive outlook has been key to my success in living a frugal lifestyle. When I focus on what I can do instead of what I can't, I find that I'm much happier and fulfilled. I'm grateful for the things I have, and I look for ways to enjoy life without breaking the bank. And when I achieve a financial goal, I take a moment to celebrate it and remind myself of how far I've come.

Living a frugal lifestyle can be challenging, but it can also be incredibly rewarding. By maintaining a positive outlook and focusing on the benefits, you'll be able to enjoy a fulfilling life while also saving money and living sustainably.

The Power of Gratitude in a Frugal Lifestyle

Living a frugal lifestyle can be challenging at times. It requires discipline, determination, and a willingness to make sacrifices. It can be easy to become focused on what you don't have, rather than what you do have. This is why gratitude is such an important part of a frugal lifestyle. When you focus on what you have, rather than what you don't have, you begin to see the abundance in your life.

Gratitude is the act of being thankful for what you have, regardless of how big or small it may be. It's about recognizing the good in your life, even during difficult times. When you practice gratitude regularly, you begin to notice how much you have to be thankful for, and this can have a powerful impact on your life.

One of the most significant benefits of practicing gratitude is that it helps you to maintain a positive outlook on life. When you focus on what you have, rather than what you lack, you're less likely to feel stressed, anxious, or unhappy. You begin to appreciate the simple things in life, such as a warm meal, a roof over your head, and the love of family and friends.

Practicing gratitude can also help you to make better financial decisions. When you're grateful for what you have, you're less likely to feel the need to spend money on things that you don't need. You become more mindful of your spending and more intentional about your purchases. You begin to focus on the things that are most important to you, rather than getting caught up in the consumerist culture.

When you're grateful for what you have, you're also more likely to take care of the things you own. You appreciate the value of the things you have and are less likely to take them for granted. This can save you money in the long run because you'll need to replace things less frequently.

One of the best ways to practice gratitude is to keep a gratitude journal. Every day, write down at least three things that you're grateful for. These can be big or small things, such as a beautiful sunset, a kind gesture from a friend, or a delicious meal. Over time, you'll begin to see how much you have to be grateful for.

Another way to practice gratitude is to express your thanks to the people in your life. Take the time to thank your loved ones for the things they do for you. This can be as simple as saying "thank you" for cooking dinner or doing the laundry. When you show appreciation for the people in your life, you'll deepen your relationships and create a more positive environment.

In conclusion, gratitude is an essential part of a frugal lifestyle. It helps you to maintain a positive outlook on life, make better financial decisions, take care of the things you own, and deepen your relationships. By practicing gratitude regularly, you'll begin to see the abundance in your life and appreciate the things that truly matter.

Coping with Setbacks and Financial Emergencies

As much as we try to plan and save for the future, unexpected setbacks and financial emergencies can still occur. It's important to be prepared and have a plan for coping with these situations without derailing our financial progress. In this chapter, we will explore some practical tips for coping with setbacks and financial emergencies while maintaining a frugal lifestyle.

The first step in dealing with a financial emergency is to stay calm and assess the situation. Take some time to gather all the information and figure out what your options are. Depending on the nature of the emergency, there may be some immediate steps you can take to minimize the damage. For example, if you suddenly lose your job, you can apply for unemployment benefits or look for temporary work to make ends meet.

It's also important to have an emergency fund in place. This can be a separate savings account that you contribute to regularly or simply a designated portion of your overall savings. The general rule of thumb is to have at least three to six months' worth of living expenses saved up for emergencies. This can give you a buffer to cover unexpected expenses and bills without having to dip into your regular savings or resort to credit cards.

If you do need to use credit to cover an emergency expense, it's important to do so strategically. Look for low-interest credit options such as personal loans or credit cards with a

0% introductory APR. Avoid using high-interest credit options such as payday loans or cash advances, which can quickly spiral out of control and make your financial situation worse.

Another way to cope with setbacks and emergencies is to prioritize your spending. Take a hard look at your budget and determine which expenses are absolutely necessary and which ones can be cut back. For example, you may need to temporarily cut back on eating out or entertainment expenses until you get back on your feet.

When facing a setback or emergency, it's also important to reach out for support. This can come in many forms, from emotional support from friends and family to professional financial advice. Don't be afraid to ask for help when you need it.

I have faced setbacks and financial emergencies in my own life, and I know firsthand how stressful and overwhelming they can be. When I was first starting out as a writer, I had to live on a shoestring budget and had very little savings. One winter, my apartment's heating system broke down, and I was faced with a hefty repair bill. I didn't have an emergency fund at the time, so I had to get creative with my budget. I cut back on all non-essential expenses, including food, and took on some extra freelance work to make ends meet. It was a difficult time, but I learned a lot from the experience and was ultimately able to recover financially.

In conclusion, setbacks and financial emergencies are a part of life, but they don't have to derail your frugal lifestyle. By staying calm, being prepared, and seeking support when you need it, you can weather these challenges and continue on your path towards financial stability. Remember to always prioritize your spending, look for low-interest credit options, and keep a positive outlook.

Celebrating the Benefits of Frugalism

As frugal living gains in popularity, it's easy to see why so many people are turning to it as a way to improve their lives. Not only can it help you save money, but it can also make you more mindful and appreciative of the things you have. In this chapter, we'll explore the many benefits of frugalism and how to celebrate them.

One of the most obvious benefits of frugalism is the amount of money you can save. By being mindful of your spending and making intentional choices about where you put your money, you can stretch your budget further than you ever thought possible. This can help you pay off debt, build up an emergency fund, and work towards your financial goals. Celebrate your savings by setting up a budget that works for you, and rewarding yourself when you hit your milestones.

Another benefit of frugalism is that it can help you simplify your life. When you focus on experiences and relationships over material possessions, you'll find that you have more time and energy for the things that matter most. By cutting out excess clutter and streamlining your routines, you can create more space in your life for the things that truly bring you joy. Celebrate your simplicity by taking a weekend to declutter and organize your home, or by finding new ways to simplify your daily routine.

Frugalism can also help you become more mindful and intentional in your choices. When you're constantly seeking the next new thing or keeping up with the Joneses, it's easy to lose sight of what truly matters to you. But when you embrace a frugal lifestyle, you're forced to be more thoughtful and intentional about your choices. You'll find that you're more aware of the things that truly bring you joy, and more conscious of the impact your choices have on the world around you. Celebrate your mindfulness by taking time to reflect on your choices and actions, and by being more present in the moment.

Conclusion

As we come to the end of this book on frugal living, I hope that you have gained valuable insights on how to live a financially sustainable and fulfilling life. Throughout the chapters, we have explored different aspects of frugalism, from budgeting and debt management to minimalism, sustainable living, and gratitude. We have discussed the importance of setting realistic financial goals, and explored the power of gratitude and positivity in a frugal lifestyle.

Through it all, you may have come to realize that frugal living is not just about pinching pennies or making do with less. It's about finding joy and fulfillment in the things that truly matter and realizing that money is a tool to help us achieve our goals and live our best lives.

As I reflect on my own journey towards frugal living, I am reminded of the many benefits that come with this lifestyle. By embracing frugality, I have been able to save money for the things that truly matter, such as travel, experiences, and investing in my future. I have also found greater peace and contentment in the simple things, such as spending time with loved ones, pursuing hobbies and interests, and appreciating the beauty of nature.

But above all, I have found that frugal living has given me a sense of freedom and empowerment. By taking control of my finances, I have been able to make choices that align with my values and goals, rather than being driven by societal pressures or consumerism.

I hope that this book has inspired you to embark on your own frugal journey, and that you have found practical tips and personal stories that resonate with your own experiences. Whether you are just starting out or have been living frugally for some time, I encourage you to continue learning, exploring, and finding joy in the process.

Remember that frugal living is not a one-size-fits-all solution, and that everyone's journey will be different. But by cultivating a mindset of gratitude, embracing the power of community and support, and focusing on the things that truly matter, I believe that we can all achieve greater financial freedom, fulfillment, and happiness.

So go forth with confidence, my friends, and embrace the many benefits of frugal living. May your journey be filled with joy, discovery, and new possibilities.

Dear Reader,

I hope you enjoyed reading this book as much as I enjoyed writing it. Thank you for taking the time to explore the world of frugal living with me.

If you found this book helpful, I would be so grateful if you could leave a positive review. Your feedback is invaluable and will help others discover the joys of frugal living.

Remember, every small step counts. By embracing a frugal lifestyle, we can live more sustainably and mindfully, while also creating a secure financial future for ourselves.

Thank you once again for reading, and I hope to hear your thoughts soon.

Best regards,

Hazel